awaken

awaken

FROM DRY BONES
TO THE RIVER OF LIFE

J. D. Walt

Printed in the United States of America

Cover and page design by Strange Last Name
Page layout by PerfecType, Nashville, Tennessee

Walt, John David.
  Awaken : from dry bones to the river of life / J.D. Walt. – Frankin, Tennessee : Seedbed Publishing, ©2018. Second edition.

  pages ; cm. – (Awakening series ; volume 1)

  ISBN 9781628246315 (paperback)
  ISBN 9781628246469 (Mobi)
  ISBN 9781628246476 (ePub)
  ISBN 9781628246483 (uPDF)

  1. Devotional calendars. 2. Bible. Ezekiel—Meditations. 3. Religious awakening--Christianity. I. Title. II. Series.

BV4810.W347 2018   260   2018955898

 Seedbed

SEEDBED PUBLISHING
Franklin, Tennessee
seedbed.com

CONTENTS

why discipleship bands?

In his final hours, Jesus prayed specifically for us, "that all of them may be one, Father, just as you are in me and I am in you. May they also be in us so that the world may believe that you have sent me" (John 17:21).

Jesus prayed for the relationships between his followers to be of the very same character of the relationships between Father, Son, and Holy Spirit. Further, he prayed that our relationships would themselves find their home within the relationships of Father, Son, and Holy Spirit. Finally, note why this matters so much. Our relationships with each other will either lead people closer to God or further away.

Why discipleship bands? Because banded discipleship creates the context for the supernatural love of God to become real in our lives and through our relationships for the world. Discipleship bands all at once create space for inward transformation and outward mission.

The great tragedy of Christian discipleship is that it has come to mean so many things it can mean next to nothing. To be sure, there are complexities to discipleship, but at the core we must have deep clarity. In his final instructions to us, Jesus made it clear:

> *"All authority in heaven and on earth has been given to me. Therefore go and make disciples of all nations, baptizing them in the name of the Father and of the Son and of the Holy Spirit, and teaching them to obey everything I have commanded you. And surely I am with you always, to the very end of the age."* (MATT. 28:18-20)

We are to make disciples and teach them to obey everything Jesus has commanded us.

Let's be clear. We are not talking about a new small-group program, or better accountability groups, or Bible study groups. We do not fail at the mission of God in the world for lack of more information or better content or enhanced skills. We fail for a lack of love. Our foremost challenge is not learning more but loving more.

We like the way our friend Phil Meadows describes discipleship bands:

> *A band is a form of fellowship that is a means of charismatic encounter with the presence, leading, and power of the Holy Spirit. We come together. Jesus Christ is present as he has promised and he breathes his Spirit powerfully. And we come to help one another fix our eyes on him, in our midst. And we come to help one another open wide our mouths to receive the Spirit he gives. And we come to have holy conversation.*

The success of the gospel of Jesus Christ rises and falls on the strength of the relationships among his followers. Jesus' ambition is not to create a bunch of autonomous individual miracle workers. His mission is to create miraculous communities. This happens very simply through the arduous journey of people learning to love one another in the very same way that the Father and the Son and the Holy Spirit love one another.

There's nothing new here. It's actually quite ancient. From Jesus' band of disciples to the present day, everywhere the church has flourished some manner of banded discipleship was at the heart of it.

Most of us aren't lazy in our faith. We are stuck. It is not that we lack commitment. We are simply arrested in our development. The way forward is as close as a few other people who are willing to band together.

what is a
discipleship band?

A discipleship band is a group of three to five people who read together, pray together, and meet together to become the love of God for one another and the world.

Carefully consider this visionary text of Scripture from Paul's letter to the Ephesians.

> *I pray that out of his glorious riches he may strengthen you with power through his Spirit in your inner being, so that Christ may dwell in your hearts through faith. And I pray that you, being rooted and established in love, may have power, together with all the Lord's holy people, to grasp how wide and long and high and deep is the love of Christ, and to know this love that surpasses knowledge— that you may be filled to the measure of all the fullness of God.* (3:16-19)

First, note this is the Word of God. Second, it is a prayer. Third, it is all about relationships. For these reasons and more, it serves as a foundational text for our work. Discipleship bands provide a context where we can do these three things well. We read together. We pray together. We meet together. And we do these things with the all-consuming goal of being "filled to the measure of all the fullness of God." This is the way toward becoming the love of God for one another and the world.

WHY SO SMALL?

It's not that reading and praying and meeting can't happen in a larger group. The point of a discipleship band is the depth and quality of discipleship possible in a micro-community model. In truth, there are only so many people one can connect with on this level of intentionality. When it comes time to meet together, it is most effective to allot at least twenty minutes for each person (to share and be prayed for). In our experience, five member bands are not advisable; two-hour meetings become difficult to manage.

WHY SAME GENDER?

While sin is common to the human race, at times it takes on different character and qualities when it comes to different genders. Because of the way shame accompanies sin it can give rise to complicated dynamics between women and men. On the one hand, mixed gender groups can hinder vulnerability because of the presence of shame. On the other hand, vulnerable sharing can create inappropriate bonding. A discipleship band must be an ever-growing place of safety, where shame can be shed and truth can be told. Anything that tends to hinder this should be avoided. While mixed gender bands are permissible, in our judgment they are not advisable.

WHY SO SIMPLE?

Small groups satisfy many needs across the span of one's life. Discipleship bands provide a focused context for depth discipleship over a significant span of time. They aren't intended to be mission or service oriented. They aim to prepare people for mission by causing the mission of the gospel to become more deeply realized in one's own life.

Discipleship begins with understanding what God has done for us. It moves to God doing this work in us. Finally, it matures as God does this work through us in the world. Many programmatic models skip over the second phase, moving people from an understanding of what God has done for us to people doing something for God. The big challenge of discipleship centers around the work of God in us.

Because it's easier to measure and report outside activity, and because it is so difficult to measure the transformation of one's deepest self, and because there is so much desperate need all around us, it is tempting to skip the inside work and cut straight to the action part. Lest we establish a false dichotomy, let's be clear—discipleship is both inside and outside. The established tendency has been to skip the former to get to the latter, resulting in a brand of mission work that is helpful but shallow, well-intentioned but self-interested.

WHY SO DIFFICULT?

Most of us are arrested in our discipleship development. We get stuck repeating the same patterns of sin. We have believed lies about God and ourselves and they hold us like a prison with bars we can't see. Depth discipleship is hard because human beings have an unfortunate and almost infinite propensity to deceive themselves. The prophet Jeremiah said it best.

> *The human heart is the most deceitful of all things, and desperately wicked. Who really knows how bad it is?*
> (JER. 17:9 NLT)

Despite our best intentions, the reason we are stuck is we do not have the kinds of relationships it takes to catalyze and sustain the kind of work the Holy Spirit wills to do in our lives. This kind of soul work requires an ever-growing honesty with oneself; the kind of honesty that is next to impossible apart from a few other people alongside. It is why we must band together.

what do
discipleship bands do?

1. Bands Read Together

The grass withers, the flower fades, but the word of our God will stand forever. (ISA. 40:8 ESV)

We are a people of One Book. The Word of God is both our constitution and compass. Though a discipleship band is not a Bible study group, one of the ways we band together is through reading a common text. John Wesley once famously wrote this stinging admonition in a letter to a certain Mr. John Premboth.

> *Whether you like it or not, read and pray daily. It is for your life; there is no other way; else you will be a trifler all your days, and a petty, superficial preacher. Do justice to your own soul; give it time and means to grow. Do not starve yourself any longer. Take up your cross and be a Christian altogether. Then will all children of God rejoice (not grieve) over you in particular.*[1]

---

1   Taken from an editorial by J. B. Chapman in *The Preacher's Magazine* (vol. 6, no. 1, January 1, 1931). The note was written to John Premboth on August 17, 1760.

There are many ways to go about reading together. What matters is finding a way to get on the same page of Scripture together. Our common text does not function as the center-piece of the band, rather it serves in a circumferential fashion to further band the group together.

2. Bands Pray Together

Devote yourselves to prayer, being watchful and thankful. (COL. 4:2)

Our commitment is to watch over one another in love, to be for one another, and to encourage one another and build each other up. Our ongoing prayer life is a fundamental and foundational way we nurture these commitments. Band mates are prayer partners. We pray together in our weekly meeting, but even when we lift one another up throughout the week, we are, in effect, praying together. Over time band mates will know one another in extraordinary ways and will develop the capacity to pray for each other like few others in our lives can.

Every week in the band meeting, each person will have an opportunity to pray for another and to be prayed for. These times of prayer, perhaps more than anything else, will serve to strengthen the bonds of the band in deeply meaningful ways.

3. Bands Meet Together

Let us hold unswervingly to the hope we profess, for he who promised is faithful. And let us consider how we may spur one another on toward love and good deeds, not giving up meeting together, as some are in the habit of doing, but encouraging one another—and all the more as you see the Day approaching. (HEB. 10:23-25)

A discipleship band has not banded together until it is regularly meeting together. Meeting together is the most critical component of the discipleship band experience. Finding a time when everyone can consistently meet together can be challenging, but in our experience, a consistent time each week works best.

Aim for four meetings a month, but you can settle for a minimum of three. If it slips to two, the meeting time should be reconsidered. This highlights the problem with setting a meeting frequency of less than weekly. Meetings inevitably get cancelled, and when this happens within a bi-weekly or monthly approach it hurts the efficacy of the band.

Meeting together can take on a variety of formats. Face-to-face is obviously the best option, but a video-chat or phone call also works fine. Some bands find themselves all living in different places, making a face-to-face meeting impossible. They meet by conference call or video-chat and work toward an annual in-person retreat together. The point is to do what works and whatever it takes.

"Again, truly I tell you that if two of you on earth agree about anything they ask for, it will be done for them by my Father in heaven. For where two or three gather in my name, there am I with them." (MATT. 18:19-20)

how to use this book

You hold in your hands a resource designed specifically for a discipleship band. It facilitates the threefold work of a band to read together, pray together, and meet together. It is recommended for band members to read one of the entries each day, allowing it to guide your praying for one another and otherwise keep you reading a common text. Keep in mind, this is not meant to be a study curriculum proper. These readings are not meant to be the centerpiece of the weekly meeting but rather they are meant to keep a band on the same page throughout the week. Perhaps it will provide fodder for a group's informal interactions in any given week. Your band can elect to cover anywhere from five to seven readings per week at your own discretion.

On page 66 of this book you'll find a guide to conduct the discipleship band meeting, which you will find helpful as you meet together.

awaken

DAY 1

the journey of awakening

LORD, I have heard of your fame; I stand in awe of your deeds, LORD. Repeat them in our day, in our time make them known; in wrath remember mercy. (HAB. 3:2)

This study is an invitation to the people of God to band together and sow for a great awakening. Not a passing revival, or a spiritual renewal, or a refreshing, but a full-scale awakening. It's time for us to recognize that as essential as our institutions of governing, education, and healing are to our world, they lack even the combined capacity to provide for the desperate needs all around us. Only a broadscale, comprehensive awakening to the mercy, grace, and all-powerful love of God can ever hope to make the difference needed in our world today.

This is not a short-term project. It's time for the people of God to take the long view, calculate our coordinates, and buckle in for what may be decades of co-laboring. We have harvested where we have not sown. It is time to sow where we may never personally harvest. We will be delighted to see a full-scale great awakening in our day, but we will be content to sow the seed for the rest of our days with the sure confidence of unfathomable blessings for the generations coming behind us. The timetable does not belong to us, but to the sovereign God and

Father of our Lord, Jesus Christ. In the eighteenth century, a band of Moravians launched an effort to sow for a great awakening in the small village of Herrnhut, Germany. The prayer meeting went on for one hundred years before giving birth to what today is considered the modern missionary movement, which evangelized the entire Western world.

We live in such a historical moment now. May it be said of us years hence, "They heard the call. They put their hand to the plow. And they never looked back."

It's time to band together again. The time has come to sow for a great awakening.

PRAY FOR ONE ANOTHER

Come Holy Spirit and interpret to me this invitation to sow for a great awakening. Confirm in my deepest soul the urgency of the world's need for you. Bring me to new awareness of my own desperate need for you. I freely yield myself to you as a willing vessel to be made an agent of awakening for the glory of your name. Amen.

CONFERENCE TOGETHER

Are you ready to sow for a great awakening? What about now brings you to readiness?

Are you ready to band together with a few others for this high calling? Share why you think it matters to walk this way together.

DAY 2

when the time is right
for awakening

In my thirtieth year, in the fourth month on the fifth day, while I was among the exiles by the Kebar River, the heavens were opened and I saw visions of God. (EZEK. 1:1)

There are three dimensions of time: the realm of eternity, which is outside of time; chronos time, which is sequential time on the clock and calendar; and kairos time, which is a moment, period, or extended season of significance. Whereas chronos time is quantitative, kairos time is qualitative.

Kairos time happens when the realm of the eternal, which is outside of time, breaks in on chronological time. Jesus came declaring a new age of awakening when he said, "The time has come . . . The kingdom of God has come near. Repent and believe the good news!" (Mark 1:15). The Greek word for time there is *kairos*. The eternal realm, "the kingdom of God," broke in on the every day, as God revealed himself in a most extraordinary fashion.

In today's text, the prophet Ezekiel speaks of a kairos season. He gives us a date on the calendar. It was the fifth day of the fourth month of his thirtieth year. What happened to turn this ordinary day into a kairos moment?: "the heavens were opened and I saw visions of God." The eternal realm broke in on the every day life of exiled Ezekiel as God revealed himself in an extraordinary way.

Kairos times and seasons are priceless eras when God opens a new door into a new day where he purposes to do new things. That's probably a pretty good working definition of an awakening. Awakening can happen in a relatively obscure and isolated way in an individual's life or in the life of a particular community. Awakening can also happen in a very public way on a large scale across entire nations. History calls those great awakenings.

PRAY FOR ONE ANOTHER

Come Holy Spirit and prepare the way for awakening. Open up the heavens in our time. Let your kingdom break in on our every day slumbering reality in a way that leaves us forever changed. I know I must play a part, but only you can do it. In Jesus' name, amen.

CONFERENCE TOGETHER

Can you identify a kairos moment or season in your life when God first became real to you? Remember what that was like and consider sharing some of it with your band today.

Imagine what a great awakening might look like if it happened in this country. What do you see? Compare notes with your band.

DAY 3

from the valley of dry bones
to the river of life

On the fifth of the month—it was the fifth year of the exile of King Jehoiachin—the word of the LORD came to Ezekiel the priest, the son of Buzi, by the Kebar River in the land of the Babylonians. There the hand of the LORD was on him. (EZEK. 1:2 3)

Our journey will walk us through two visions of awakening from the Old Testament. The ancient prophet Ezekiel will serve as our guide along this way of awakening. We will not take a traditional Bible-study approach to these texts; rather, we will try to see them from the vantage point of the New Testament. When we open our hearts and minds to the whole of Scripture, many deep and rich insights emerge.

Ezekiel was a prophet in exile. He did his work in unfavorable conditions, prophesying to broken and desperate refugees in Babylonian captivity. If you want to get a lay of the land ahead, read Ezekiel 37 and 47. These are two expansive visions given to Ezekiel from the Spirit of God. We know them as "the vision of the valley of dry bones" and "the vision of the river of life."

Awakening begins in a lifeless valley filled with dry bones. It comes to full fruition on the lush banks of a rushing river, bringing life wher ever it goes. The story of awakening runs an epic course from deep sleep to an awe-inspiring movement of everlasting life. Awakening begins in the land of impossible. It winds along the way of the cross. It ends in the country of eternal possibility—nothing short of resurrection life.

PRAY FOR ONE ANOTHER

Come Holy Spirit, stir in us the audacity to hope for what seems far-fetched and even impossible. Would you awaken my faith to believe in the power of hidden, small beginnings? In Jesus' name, amen.

CONFERENCE TOGETHER

Share with your band your intentions, hopes, and apprehensions about this study.

DAY 4

awakening begins with me

The hand of the LORD was on me, and he brought me out by the Spirit of the LORD and set me in the middle of a valley; it was full of bones. (EZEK. 37:1)

Awakening begins in the middle of a valley full of bones.

The mysterious miracle of awakening happens not so much on the mountain tops, but in the low places of loss, the rough places of brokenness, and in the dark places of desperate need. The valley full of bones is a vision of profound need we know we could never hope to meet.

Yes, we are first awakened in this valley of vision by an awareness of need. We often first perceive this valley of bones in the form of the great needs of people in the world around us. Certainly we live in such a time today.

But hasn't every age and generation in the history of the world been in need of an awakening to the mercy and grace of God? Yes. So why do awakenings come in some generations and ages and seemingly not in others?

Awakenings happen in eras when those of us who look out on the desperate need of our time finally realize the desperate need in ourselves. Awakenings must begin with us. No, awakening must begin with me.

I must awaken to the reality that I stand in a valley full of bones and mine are among them.

That's the hardest part, because I am pretty sure I'm already awake.

PRAY FOR ONE ANOTHER

Lord Jesus, help us to be more humble. We confess we don't know what we don't know. I know you, Lord, at one level and yet I know there are so many more levels at which to know you. Break through my stuckness. Interrupt my sleepiness. Come Holy Spirit and awaken us to more of you. We welcome it. In Jesus' name. Amen.

CONFERENCE TOGETHER

Would you share with your band a sense of what you think the Holy Spirit aspires to do in your life these days?

DAY 5

blinded by the darkness

He led me back and forth among them, and I saw a great many bones on the floor of the valley, bones that were very dry. (EZEK. 37:2)

There is a stark difference between light and darkness. The problem is what lies between: a thousand shades of dim. Rarely is the shift between light and darkness a dramatic one. It is a long process of slow and subtle dimming. We so quickly adjust our eyes to the slow dimming of the lights we can hardly perceive the change happening around us . . . until it's dark. We want to think we would recognize the darkness, but by the time it's dark we can no longer see. The problem with this process of dimming is the way it seductively brings on the blindness of sleep.

This is the valley of dry bones. It is a bed for the sleep of darkness. Entire nations and cultures can become blinded by the darkness through the slow dimming of the light.

Again, the great temptation is to believe that the blinding darkness is all out there in the valley of dry bones. We can walk back and forth among them for years, surveying the desolation and desecration of what once was. We can lament the loss of days long past. We can invoke our anger, lash out at the darkness, and cast blame for its shadows. Or we can awaken to the reality that this dark, dry desert has permeated and infected us too with the slow sleep of complacency.

The only way to resist the temptation is to invite the searching light of the Holy Spirit to survey the valley of our own souls. Darkness and dryness are only a problem to the extent we can't perceive it; to the degree we aren't asleep to them.

PRAY FOR ONE ANOTHER

Come Holy Spirit and illumine us. We are so used to who we are and how we are that we aren't clear about what's true and what's not. We don't know what we don't know. And we cannot know ourselves apart from your soul-searching light. Turn on the lights and reveal the dryness in our lives that we might learn to seek you more truly. In Jesus' name, amen.

CONFERENCE TOGETHER

What keeps us from being completely honest with each other about the quality of our souls?

DAY 6

the big question and
the bigger answer

He asked me, "Son of man, can these bones live?" I said, "Sovereign
LORD, you alone know." (EZEK. 37:3)

For awakening to come to the nations, a different kind of revival must come to the church. And for revival to come to the church, a different kind of renewal must come to many millions of men and women.

It will not be driven by our hand-wringing angst about the insurmountable challenges around us. We are talking about something beyond what present generations have known; not a mere resurgence of our resolve or even our commitment. Neither are we talking about a mere recovery of some particular kind of charismatic experience or spiritual phenomenon. And for God's sake, we are not talking about a revitalization of our bestlaid plans to grow the church—driven by our visionary leadership, strategic thinking, and enterprising programs—no matter how prayerfully conceived they may be.

We are talking about something far more primitive, a renewal of the original and eternal source of life at the core of our beings. We are talking about a profound renewal of the very life of God in the souls of men and women. Hence the fundamental question, "Can these bones live?"

We must resist our incessant impulse to answer with optimism. We must release our expectations, renounce any entitlement, and return, like so many bones, to the ground from which we came, together crying out in humble submission, "Sovereign LORD, only you know."

PRAY FOR ONE ANOTHER

Come Holy Spirit, stir up our confidence in you, strip us of our confidence in ourselves, and renew in our deepest souls a submission to your sovereignty. We confess that we do not know if these bones can live; only you do. We need something more than our thin can-do optimism going forward. We need to be filled with you. In Jesus' name, amen.

CONFERENCE TOGETHER

Of all the possible ways we might answer this question, "Can these bones live?" why must, "Sovereign LORD, only you know," be the only response? What is explicitly and implicitly implied by this response?

DAY 7

awakening fundamental #1:
the word of God

Then he said to me, "Prophesy to these bones and say to them,
'Dry bones, hear the word of the LORD!'" (EZEK. 37:4)

Now we come to the first of the two fundamental fundamentals of awakening: the Word of God and the Spirit of God. New awakenings do not come through discovering new things. No, they come from the rediscovery of first things—the primitive foundations of Word and Spirit.

By the Word of the Lord, creation was created. And by the Word of the Lord, the world is being saved. The Word of the Lord always accomplishes the purposes for which it is sent. Living and active, sharper than a double-edged sword, the Word of the Lord inspires, instructs, encourages, rebukes, and counsels, bringing down the proud and raising up the humble. It is the most fundamental form of nourishment for the human race, for we do not live by bread alone but by every word that comes from the mouth of God.

Awakening requires us to come into a different kind of relationship to the Word of the Lord. It will require setting aside some of what we think we already know—unlearning our preferred way of mastery in order that we might once again be mastered by this powerful Word. The operative words are "prophesy" and "hear." There is no shortage of the presence of the words of the Lord. There is however, as Amos prophesied, "a famine of hearing the words of the LORD" (Amos 8:11).

Before we can become the agents of awakening, we must first hear the awakening word ourselves. We must prophesy to the bones that are ourselves and one another, "Dry bones, hear the word of the LORD!" And we must hear. Let us pray for ears to hear.

PRAY FOR ONE ANOTHER

Heavenly Father, we want to speak to one another in this band in the authority of the Word of God and in the power of the Holy Spirit, saying, "Dry bones, hear the word of the LORD!" "Hear the Word of the LORD" (one name at a time). Give us ears to hear and eyes to see that we might be awakened in a deeper way to your presence in our lives and your purposes for our times. We pray in Jesus' name. Amen.

CONFERENCE TOGETHER

If your consumption of the Word of God was the only food you put into your body would you be empty, emaciated, gaining weight, satisfied, heavy, obese? Reflect on that with your band.

DAY 8

awakening fundamental #2:
the spirit of God

This is what the Sovereign Lord says to these bones: I will make breath enter you, and you will come to life. (EZEK. 37:5)

We come to the second fundamental of awakening: the Spirit of God. We have the Word of God and now we hear about the Spirit of God.

This is a new creation story isn't it? Remember in the garden of Eden we are told, "Then the Lord God formed a man from the dust of the ground and breathed into his nostrils the breath of life, and the man became a living being" (Gen. 2:7).

The Holy Spirit, the third person of the Trinity, is the breath of life. He breathes life into our lifelessness. The Holy Spirit's presence is eternal life itself. The interesting feature of breath is its on-going-ness. While a single breath means life for the next moment, that same breath will not be life for the moment after that. Note, though, this is not life support. This is life itself. As human beings we are shaped and crafted by the Word of God and raised to life by the Spirit of God. This is the prophetic Word of God to us: "I will make breath enter you and you will come to life." And as we come to life so we stay gloriously alive—by the breath of life from the Holy Spirit.

All too often, awakening (both personal and corporate) is arrested at this point. We have an infinitely high capacity for the life of the Holy Spirit in us and yet we have a desperately low reality of the Spirit's presence and power in our lives. We hear the recreating Word of God about salvation but we never fully open ourselves to the Spirit of God. Or we started well enough but over time our breathing has grown shallow. Perhaps we find ourselves at a place where we know it's time to learn to breathe more deeply than we ever have before.

Awakening grows as our reality starts moving again toward our possibility.

Perhaps we need to stretch toward prophesying over one another. To prophesy is to speak the Word of the Lord with the same Spirit and authority by which it was inspired. To prophesy is to boldly declare the living, working Word of the Lord in faith. It means to speak to the things that are not as though they already were.

PRAY FOR ONE ANOTHER

Heavenly Father, we want to speak to one another in this band in the authority of the Word of God and in the power of the Holy Spirit, saying, "Hear the Word of the Lord, [one name at a time], 'I will make breath enter you, and you will come to life.'" And now I open myself to this reality of your Spirit like never before. Awaken us to the reality of your possibility in our lives. We pray in Jesus' name, amen.

CONFERENCE TOGETHER

What holds people back from the fullness of life and breath by the power of the Holy Spirit? What holds you back?

DAY 9

awakening is not
spiritual self-improvement

"I will attach tendons to you and make flesh come upon you and cover you with skin; I will put breath in you, and you will come to life. Then you will know that I am the LORD." (EZEK. 37:6)

The miracle of awakening can never be reduced to spiritual renewal, good as that may be. This must be Word and Spirit, body and soul, heart and hands. As Scripture declares, "And if the Spirit of him who raised Jesus from the dead is living in you, he who raised Christ from the dead will also give life to your mortal bodies because of his Spirit who lives in you" (Rom. 8:11).

What does this mean? Awakening is not a touch from God, as though all that were needed was a bit of healing and renewal. No, awakening is a totalizing invasion and infusion of Word and Spirit, the present inbreaking of the realm and ultimate reality of eternal life. We are not talking about the renovation of an old house into a better house. We speak not of renewal of life but the resurrection from death; dead bones coming to life. This is not a spiritual self-improvement program. This is a comprehensive shifting of the center of gravity in our lives, from sin and death to love and life.

The Word of God wills to be made flesh—to take on human skin. The Spirit of God wills to be made breath, filling mortal bodies with miraculous life. No, awakening cannot be reduced to mere spiritual renewal.

It happens when Word and Spirit come together to make gloriously visible the will of God in the working of human beings.

When the unseen is once again visualized, the knowledge about God turns into the palpable knowing, as in, "Then you will know that I am the LORD."

PRAY FOR ONE ANOTHER

Lord Jesus, awaken us (name band members) and awaken me. I open my life to a totalizing and ongoing infusion of Word and Spirit and welcome the fullness of Jesus Christ through the life, presence, and power of the Holy Spirit in me. I confess I have and am settling for less than your best. I will be patient to seek you and to wait for you as long as it takes. It is in the power of and for the sake of your name I pray, Jesus. Amen.

CONFERENCE TOGETHER

What would happen if this "coming to life" kind of awakening began to occur more and more in my local church or campus ministry? Take it a step further. What would happen if this began to happen at my place of work or in my school?

DAY 10

awakening happens
suddenly and slowly

---

*So I prophesied as I was commanded. And as I was prophesying,
there was a noise, a rattling sound, and the bones came together,
bone to bone.* (EZEK. 37:7)

Awakening does not happen all at once. It comes in stages and
grows by degrees. We like to reference the contrast of night and
day while forgetting the similarities of evening and morning.
Still, evening and morning are two quite differing phenomena.
Just as night falls by the slow descent of the sun beneath the
horizon, morning breaks well before the sun makes its appear-
ance over the land. Remember, darkness comes slowly and by
shades well after the sun itself disappears. Sunsets leave a bril-
liance of slowly fading color, leaving us with a last and even
nostalgic remembrance of days gone by. Darkness comes by
a slow fade. Morning rises by a slow growing light and at the
right moment, the sun breaks the horizon with the luminosity
of a thousand blazing fires.

There are always many more people to gaze at the sunset
than those who gather to await the sunrise. Many who seek
an awakening make the mistake of asking the Lord to, "do that

again," longing for the return of days gone by. Sunsets give us a self-satisfied gratitude for the day past but they do not increase our anticipation for the next sunrise.

Bones do not appear until after the long slow rot of decomposition. It takes even longer for bones to detach and dry out. Why do we think everything will come back together in response to a few prayerful meetings? In this age of technological wonder, where everything is immediate, have we come to believe we can flip the switch on awakening?

There's a seductive form of revivalism that believes if we do a, b, and c that God will be forced to do x, y, and z. After all, that's how it worked before. Right?

Wrong. To sow for awakening means coming to the sobering awareness that God owes us nothing and there's nothing we can do to somehow get God in our debt. The Lord is searching for a generation of sunrise people; those whose hearts are completely his—come what may—and who have the audacity to be forerunners of the morning, the courage to awaken the dawn.

PRAY FOR ONE ANOTHER

Sovereign Lord, only you know if these bones can live. It is in your hands and yet we will not cease crying out to you. We know you aren't looking for some kind of fervency in the form of our prayers. You are looking for your own brokenhearted love for lost generations to rise up in us. Let that be the measure of our fervency. Lord Jesus, awaken your brokenhearted holy love in us that we might be part of that sunrise generation on the horizon. For your sake and in your name we pray. Amen.

CONFERENCE TOGETHER

Are you more of a sunset person or a sunrise person? How do you understand the difference when it comes to sowing for awakening? Where do you hear even the faintest echoes of that rattling sound bones make when they are starting to come back together? How about your band—are there signs of awakening emerging among you?

DAY 11

the necessity of breath

I looked, and tendons and flesh appeared on them and skin covered them, but there was no breath in them. (EZEK. 37:8)

We want awakening to come suddenly, accompanied by signs, wonders, and spectacular movement. This is what gets remembered from days of old. As a consequence, we want the sunrise without the long labor of a thousand night watches. We want the awe of transformation without the agony of travail. We want the mountain-top view without the years spent in the valley of vision.

It's why we've settled for far too many wake-up calls that stopped short of awakenings. For a body to come together from a pile of bones is an unimaginable, awe-inspiring sight. It is not enough. A body without breath remains asleep. We all too easily settle for the signs of awakening without pressing further into it. It's like being awakened by an alarm clock only to repeatedly hit the snooze bar.

The Word of God without the Spirit of God produces a form of reality without the power. On the other hand, the Spirit of God without the Word of God brings fire without any form. The Word of God will put tendons and flesh on bones and even the covering of skin, but without the Spirit of God there remains no breath of life.

Have we been content to consider belief in the truth of the tenets of faith as faith itself—believing in the Word of God without breathing in the Spirit of God? This leaves us with a kind of listlessness—a form of religion without the power. It is the tragedy of equating easy belief with true awakening. We must press further.

PRAY FOR ONE ANOTHER

Sovereign Lord, we are tired because we have learned to believe more than we have learned to breathe. Disciple us in the way of Jesus that we might learn to breathe deeply of the Holy Spirit. Our breathing is far to shallow to sustain the kind of awakening you bring: Word and Spirit; body and breath; form and power. We need the Word of God not just to be the truth for us but the truth in us. Only your Spirit can bring that about. Come Holy Spirit! In Jesus' name, amen.

CONFERENCE TOGETHER

How about me? Am I believing without breathing? Is my breathing shallow? What would it mean to increase my lung capacity, so to speak?

DAY 12

awakening the saved
from their sleep

*Then he said to me, "Prophesy to the breath; prophesy, son of man,
and say to it, 'This is what the Sovereign LORD says: Come, breath,
from the four winds and breathe into these slain, that they may
live.'"* (EZEK. 37:9)

Come Holy Spirit! There is no awakening apart from the Holy
Spirit. Without the Holy Spirit there will be forms of religion
without the power, duty without desire, discipline without
delight, knowledge without knowing, and, yes, bodies
without breath.

We live in an age where even the so-called saved can still
be asleep. We have made it all too easy to accept the terms of
salvation like we would accept the licensing agreement on
a piece of software. So many have quietly lamented in their
souls that there must be more than this, while the machinery
of church churns on.

Perhaps the awakening we who are in the church need is an
awakening to the infinite more-ness of the gospel. We have
walked through the door without moving our lives into the

house. We have been lulled into contentedness, satisfied to have a key to the home without actually living there.

We must prophesy to the breath, "Come Holy Spirit 'and breathe into these slain, that they may live.'" Perhaps more important, we must prophesy to the breath, "Come Holy Spirit and breathe into these souls who have been saved by grace yet are still hitting the snooze bar."

Writing in the midst of a great awakening in the nineteenth century, Edwin Hatch wrote the hymn, "Breathe on Me Breath of God." The hymn speaks to the progressive nature of awakening. We will shape our praying today with the third stanza.

PRAY FOR ONE ANOTHER

Breathe on me, breath of God, till I am wholly thine, till all this earthly part of me glows with thy fire divine. We confess, we believe more than we breathe. We need your breath or we remain mere bodies; busy, to be sure, but breathless. Touch us with your truth in such a way that our lives become truly alive. We long for this. In Jesus' name, amen.

CONFERENCE TOGETHER

What holds me back from breathing deeply of the Holy Spirit? Lack of understanding? Fear? Lack of faith? Indifference? Share your answers with your band.

DAY 13

awakening begins with the house of God

So I prophesied as he commanded me, and breath entered them; they came to life and stood up on their feet—a vast army. (EZEK. 37:10)

Perhaps the most critical reality of this visionary text is who it references. This awakening of the dry bones in the valley of vision is not referring to the unbelieving world at large. This text is about an awakening of the very people of God, the house of Israel.

As noted on a prior day, we so readily see the profound need for great awakening in the surrounding society. It is much harder to see our own need of it. This will require a new kind of humility of us—a recognition of the gap between who we are and who Jesus aspires for us to become.

Can we shed all pretense and become honest with one another about the slumbering of our own souls, which is manifest in our readiness to excuse our own sin while calling out the faults of others?

Can we slay our spiritual pride and confess to one another that there is so much more of the Word of God and the Spirit of God that we have yet to grasp? And can we lock arms in the interest of helping one another reach these new depths of life and love?

It is time for us, the people of God, to prophesy one to another—to gather in small circles of covenant faith where we might prophesy to the bones and to the breath for the sake of a greater awakening among us. As Scripture says, let judgment begin with the house of God (see 1 Peter 4:17), we in like fashion say, let awakening begin with the house of God.

PRAY FOR ONE ANOTHER

Lord Jesus Christ, we have seen the bones and the bones are us. Increase our hunger for your Word and our thirst for your Spirit. Birth a new beginning in us, in me, for the sake of your great name being known in all the earth. Help us believe in a new way—the way that leads to the deep breathing of the Holy Spirit in us. Whether we think we are slumbering or not, we can agree that there is far more of you we have yet to know. Come Holy Spirit and awaken me and (name your band members) that we might become the agents of awakening for others. In your name, Jesus, amen.

CONFERENCE TOGETHER

Where am I in the journey of awakening? Asleep? Still hitting the snooze bar? Out of bed? Getting dressed? Hungry for the Word? Thirsty for the Spirit? Rising up in the brokenhearted holy love of God for the sleeping world? Choose one that describes you and share some reflection with your band.

DAY 14

from vain grandeur to
humble beginnings

---

*Then he said to me: "Son of man, these bones are the people of
Israel. They say, 'Our bones are dried up and our hope is gone; we
are cut off.'"* (EZEK. 37:11)

Indeed, these bones are your bones and these bones are my
bones. Yes, let awakening begin with the house of God. But
how? Many millions of Jesus' faithful followers feel cut off
from the great movement of the church Jesus founded. We
faithfully go to church yet feel distant from the global movement of the Holy Spirit. We want to jump into the current of
the great river of God but we are bound in a valley of dry bones.
What matters most now?

Obedience matters—a lot. The waves of awakening will ride
on the churn of humble, bold obedience. Dr. Dennis Kinlaw, a
great man of faith, witnessed a profound awakening at Asbury
College in 1970 (one whose waves have not ceased). Reflecting
decades later on what preceded the great outpouring of God's
Spirit, he remarked, "God never does anything in a big way that
he doesn't first do in a small way."

Aspiring for an awakening can quickly turn into vain grandeur. Our minds readily turn to big things. In reality, awakenings mostly begin when a few ordinary people, often in obscurity, band together and move boldly in the ways of small, steadfast obedience. Prophesying to the bones and the breath begins not in public demonstration but in hidden prayer. A growing crowd will not be the first sign of this awakening. The world will know awakening is afoot when hundreds and then thousands and then hundreds of thousands of small circles of threes and fours and fives band together for the long haul to sow for a great awakening. You and I will know it has begun when we put our own hands to this plow and vow to never look back.

PRAY FOR ONE ANOTHER

Father, I pray for the audacity to prophesy; to breathe deep of the Holy Spirit and declare the promising, powerful Word of God over the lives of others. I want to be one who humbly prophesies awakening. Teach our band to prophesy to the bones and prophesy to the breath for the sake of one another. I pray in your name, Jesus. Amen.

CONFERENCE TOGETHER

How can our band pray and prophesy awakening faith over one another? What holds us back from doing so?

DAY 15

between the two
greatest awakenings

Therefore prophesy and say to them: 'This is what the Sovereign LORD says: My people, I am going to open your graves and bring you up from them; I will bring you back to the land of Israel. Then you, my people, will know that I am the LORD, when I open your graves and bring you up from them. I will put my Spirit in you and you will live, and I will settle you in your own land. Then you will know that I the LORD have spoken, and I have done it, declares the LORD.' (EZEK. 37:12-14)

Resurrection. It's the most powerful word in the entire Bible, yet because of its familiarity to us we pass right by it. Resurrection. It means to raise the dead from the grave never to die again. This is the ultimate and fullest and final awakening—the most unbelievable, unfathomable, and, yes, impossible thing in the world.

And it has already happened. It's underway. It goes like this: on the third day he arose from the dead.

And because Jesus is raised from the dead, we too will be raised from the dead, when he comes in the fullness of his kingdom. We declare it in our creeds and proclaim it from our Scriptures.

"But Christ has indeed been raised from the dead, the first-fruits of those who have fallen asleep. For since death came through a man, the resurrection of the dead comes also through a man. For as in Adam all die, so in Christ all will be made alive" (1 Cor. 15:20–22). We live between these great awakenings: the resurrection of Jesus Christ from the dead and the resurrection of the dead at the end of the age. Every awakening is an echo of the resurrection of Jesus and a fore-shadowing of the great resurrection to come.

By the miraculous mercy of God, we now walk in the power of the resurrection as agents of awakening, standing on the promise living in its fulfillment.

PRAY FOR ONE ANOTHER

Almighty God and Father, thank you for raising your Son, Jesus, from the dead, and thank you for the promise that you will one day raise us from the dead. And thank you for filling us with the life-raising power of your Holy Spirit. I ask you to awaken us to more of your resurrection life, love, and power. I pray in the name of Jesus, amen.

CONFERENCE TOGETHER

Have you gone to sleep on the significance and power of the word "resurrection"? Are you waking up to the truth and power of resurrection life in a new way? Share with your band.

DAY 16

awakening fundamental #3:
the house of God

The man brought me back to the entrance to the temple, and I saw water coming out from under the threshold of the temple toward the east (for the temple faced east). The water was coming down from under the south side of the temple, south of the altar. (EZEK. 47:1)

Awakening always means reorientation with first things and fundamental truths. We have talked about the preeminence of the Word of God and the priority of the Spirit of God. Today, we come back to the fundamental truths of the house of God.

It's important, though, at the outset that we not confuse house of God with a building. It is so easy to make the leap from the Old Testament temple to the New Testament church and to equate temple and church as specific, fixed places. The house of God is now the church and the church is the people of God. We must let go of our thinking that awakening must happen in the building we call the church. Sure, our gatherings in our church buildings are important but they are neither the source of awakening nor the means of its spread.

Now is the time to recover this truth: the house of God is the people of God. The people of God are the temple of the Holy

Spirit. As long our idea of house equals a building, we will be limited to thinking awakening happens somewhere other than here at some other time than this.

When the Word of God meets the Spirit of God in the midst of the people of God we have the essential ingredients of awakening.

PRAY FOR ONE ANOTHER

Come Holy Spirit and impress upon us the truth that our bodies are temples of the Holy Spirit and together we are living stones being built together as a spiritual house. Put us together as a little room for your presence a place where your love and power can now into and through us for others. We ask this in Jesus' name. Amen.

CONFERENCE TOGETHER

What will it take for us to reconceive of ourselves, together, as the house of God, the temple of the Holy Spirit, and not be so locked into the church as building thinking?

DAY 17

awakening is an outside reality

He then brought me out through the north gate and led me around the outside to the outer gate facing east, and the water was trickling from the south side. (EZEK. 47:2)

Perhaps the most critical word from today's text is the word "outside." When our understanding of awakening is limited to what happens in a building our experience of awakening tends to be pretty "inside" oriented. The focus gets placed on getting people to the building.

But that's not the story of Ezekiel 47, is it? There's the source and the stream; the well and the water. It's easy to get those confused, especially to think of the source (or well) as being located in a fixed place. Indeed, the Old Testament temple was the source or the well from which this living water flowed. As we noted earlier, Jesus and his followers are the new temple of God. He is the chief cornerstone and we are the "living stones are being built up as a spiritual house" (1 Peter 2:5 ESV). Now, admittedly, all this house language is tricky, because remember, it's not about the building.

Awakening is not an inside phenomenon but an outside movement. Keep the big picture in mind. What began a valley filled with dry bones has now become the source of a flowing stream. In fact, the source, the Son of God, and the stream, the people of God, are one in the same. The miracle of awakening happens as we become part of the moving stream, which constantly bears its source of life everywhere it goes. That is what's about to happen in this story.

But don't forget. Awakening is an outside thing.

PRAY FOR ONE ANOTHER

Lord Jesus, we confess we are stuck in our thinking that church is a place we go. Open our minds and hearts to your words when you said, "I will build my church, and the gates of hell shall not prevail against" (Matt. 16:18 ESV). Show us what that church is and how you build it. Open our minds to understand not that we are the church, but that we are the "my church" you are building. Yes, Lord, we are your church—even our little band—outside, right where we are. For your name's sake, amen.

CONFERENCE TOGETHER

What holds your band back from thinking of yourselves and acting together as "little" church? What might change if you saw yourselves like this?

DAY 18

knowing vs. knowing about

As the man went eastward with a measuring line in his hand, he measured off a thousand cubits and then led me through water that was ankle-deep. (EZEK. 47:3)

Let's stay with the source and stream thought for a minute more today.

Do you remember that time Jesus stood up in the temple courts and cried out in a loud voice, "Let anyone who is thirsty come to me and drink. Whoever believes in me, as Scripture has said, rivers of living water will flow from within them" (John 7:37–38)?

That is a promise. See how that works? Jesus is the source and by the river-like movement of the Holy Spirit he dwells in us. That makes us both source and stream of living water.

Right here is where the logjams happen. So many of us are stuck at the point of the source, thinking we know God when, in reality, we only know *about* God. We have a lot of knowledge about Jesus, but when it comes down to it, we don't really know him. And so often, those who know him have drifted off to sleep and stalled out somewhere along the way. It is why we are ever in need of deeper awakening.

Back to the logjam—how does our knowing catch up with our knowledge? That's the great mystery, the secret long hidden—now revealed. Two words: Holy Spirit. Jesus, the Source, will never become the stream in and through us without our welcoming the fullness of the Holy Spirit into our lives. The Holy Spirit breaks the logjam within us, turning knowledge into knowing, quenching the eternal thirst of our souls, and making us move like a river from its source. That is a promise.

Is anyone thirsty?

It takes time. A thousand cubits can be a ways to go. We must be patient.

Ankle deep is good.

PRAY FOR ONE ANOTHER

Come Holy Spirit and break the logjam of our knowledge about you in such a way that our knowing you can grow. Yes, translate our knowledge into knowing. We know that will require deeper humility on our part, to be honest with one another about where we are. Help us with that. We pray in Jesus' name, amen.

CONFERENCE TOGETHER

Are you thirsty for more of the Holy Spirit in your life or satisfied with where you are? Has your knowing caught up with your knowledge? Reflect on this with your band.

DAY 19

from trickle to high tide

He measured off another thousand cubits and led me through water that was knee-deep. He measured off another thousand and led me through water that was up to the waist. (EZEK 47:4)

Remember the bit about awakening being an outside thing? Here's what's amazing about today's text. The further we get from the temple, the deeper the water gets. It seems like it would be just the opposite—lots of water at the source that trickles out smaller and smaller as it goes out.

The mystery of this river is the way its source moves with it. As the source moves so the stream grows. And so it goes with the work of the Holy Spirit in our lives. There is always more. Remember that time Jesus went to the wedding party in Cana—the one where they ran out of wine? Yes, Jesus turned water into wine, but not just a little bit. It came to around one hundred fifty gallons of wine, and it wasn't just okay wine. It was the very best wine. The longer the party went on the better the wine got. That is how it is with Jesus. The further down the river we go, the deeper the water gets. With Jesus, life will not get easier and easier. In fact, it will probably get harder, but it will get better and better. In fact, the best will be saved for last.

This is how awakening works in our lives and through our lives into the world. It starts as a trickle and builds slowly and steadily—now knee-deep . . . now waist-deep. This can happen in our lives over a period of weeks and months. In the wider world it can take years and even decades to build. On both fronts, that of our lives and that of the world, we must hold on to patience and perseverance. On both fronts it often takes the vantage point of years in the future to look back and understand how it happened.

PRAY FOR ONE ANOTHER

Come Holy Spirit and raise the water level in the riverbed that is our band. Save us from the isolated way of seeing ourselves as a few independent, self-sufficient people and open us up to new growth together. Let the water level rise not just in our individual selves but in our life together. Teach us the all for one and one for all way of your working. In Jesus' name, amen.

CONFERENCE TOGETHER

How would you characterize the depth of the water as a band? Ankle-deep? Knee-deep? Waist-deep? Other? How can we learn to think of ourselves more together than as apart?

DAY 20

awakening is personal experience plus public reality

He measured off another thousand, but now it was a river that I could not cross, because the water had risen and was deep enough to swim in—a river that no one could cross. (EZEK. 47:5)

There's a song from the late 1990s by Darrell Evans called "Let the River Flow." It's a song about awakening. Here are some of the lyrics:

Let the poor man say
I am rich in Him
Let the lost man say
I am found in Him
Let the river now

Let the blind man say
I can see again
Let the dead man say
I am born again
Let the river now

Awakening can never be confined to a spiritual experience. If it does not move beyond private religious experience and into public reality it is not an awakening. Awakening changes everything. Not only are people healed of all sorts of maladies, but hospitals get built. Not only are the poor lifted out of their plight, but new centers of education are established. Not only are people delivered from addictions, but drug trade diminishes. Not only do homeless people find homes, but entire new sectors of the economy open up. Mercy beyond handouts flows into the streets. True justice rings from the courthouses. Charitable contributions transform into sacrificial gifts.

Let's give the prophet Isaiah the last word today. Here's how he describes a great awakening. Allow yourself to relish these words:

The Spirit of the Sovereign LORD is on me,
  because the LORD has anointed me
  to proclaim good news to the poor.
He has sent me to bind up the brokenhearted,
  to proclaim freedom for the captives
  and release from darkness for the prisoners,
to proclaim the year of the LORD's favor
  and the day of vengeance of our God,
to comfort all who mourn,
  and provide for those who grieve in Zion—
to bestow on them a crown of beauty
  instead of ashes,
the oil of joy
  instead of mourning,
and a garment of praise
  instead of a spirit of despair.

They will be called oaks of righteousness,
  a planting of the LORD
  for the display of his splendor.

They will rebuild the ancient ruins
  and restore the places long devastated;
they will renew the ruined cities
  that have been devastated for generations.
  (ISA. 61:1-4)

That's what a river of life too wide to cross looks like.

PRAY FOR ONE ANOTHER

Come Holy Spirit and expand our notion of what awakening looks like in the world—that it is so much more than our experience. Give us concrete vision of what awakening would look like in our families and in the community and with those who are in need. We confess we tend to have our faith in a pretty tight privatized box. Get us out of that box. We pray in Jesus' name, amen.

CONFERENCE TOGETHER

Who are the poor and the brokenhearted and the captives and those who mourn in our midst? How can we begin to bend the river to reach them?

DAY 21

the perception required
to sense awakening

He asked me, "Son of man, do you see this?" (EZEK. 47:6)

"Do you see this?" That's the question.

Be mindful, Ezekiel is seeing a vision, but we must remember where sight comes from. Remember where we began: "On the fifth of the month—it was the fifth year of the exile of King Jehoiachin—the word of the LORD came to Ezekiel" (Ezek. 1:2–3).

Seeing comes from hearing—the word of the Lord came to Ezekiel. In fact, faith comes by hearing. It makes sense. Scripture says we walk by faith and not by sight. We exist in a world where seeing is believing, but we live in a kingdom that is just the opposite: believing is seeing. We hear. We believe. We see. Scripture speaks regularly about having ears to hear and eyes to see, noting how common it is to look and not see, to hear and not listen.

The Holy Spirit wills to give a new and ever-growing kind of perception to all who will humble themselves to receive it. The reason so many are so cynical about the possibilities of awakening in our day is they lack this holy kind of perception.

Cynicism comes from the defeat of idealism—which is our best vision for how things should work out. The Holy Spirit does not offer idealism. The kingdom of God is not built on utopian ideals. It's not the eradication of brokenness, but its beautification. The kingdom of heaven is the right now reality, ever hovering over the present state of affairs, waiting to break in with awakening, redemption, and the reversal of all that is broken and desecrated.

The Spirit of God awaits those who are humble enough to hear the Word of God and bold enough to speak of the vision. That's why, in the old days, the words and visions from God came to the prophets. We, however, live in the new days, the age of the Spirit. Remember what Peter proclaimed on the day of Pentecost:

In the last days, God says,
I will pour out my Spirit on all people.
Your sons and daughters will prophesy,
your young men will see visions,
your old men will dream dreams. (ACTS 2:17)

"Do you see this?" That's the question. Don't wait for the vision. Begin by believing it.

PRAY FOR ONE ANOTHER

Come Holy Spirit and open the eyes of our hearts. We want to see the unseen real. We confess we have waited to see before we would believe. Show us what it would mean for us to believe first, and to move out in action before we see. We are ready to be those kind of people—people of real faith. In Jesus' name, amen.

CONFERENCE TOGETHER

Are you ready to walk by the sight that comes by faith? Are you open to the kind of holy perception only the Holy Spirit can give? Share with your band your sense of what this means.

DAY 22

the discipleship of
the imagination

*Then he led me back to the bank of the river. When I arrived there,
I saw a great number of trees on each side of the river.* (EZEK. 47:6-7)

Trees figure very prominently in Scripture. We see them
in the beginning in the garden of Eden. We see them at the
end in the revelation of John. Isaiah speaks of the trees of
the field clapping their hands (see Isaiah 55). Note how he
describes an awakened generation, "They will be called oaks
of righteousness, a planting of the LORD for the display of his
splendor" (Isa. 61:3).

Trees are signs of flourishing.

The Psalms open up with a powerful vision of a tree next to
a river, giving us a vision of what the blessed or flourishing
life looks like. They are "like a tree planted by streams of
water, which yields its fruit in season and whose leaves do not
wither—whatever they do prospers" (Ps. 1:3). The tree is like an
immovable, powerful, and creative word. The river is the visual
representation of the invisible Spirit, the source of life. Do you
see this? Word plus Spirit equals life.

This is a vision we must begin to visualize. We must ask the Holy Spirit to take us inside of the world being recreated by the revelation of Scripture. In this world—which is the only true world—the mountains are bowing down before the Lord and the oceans are roaring with the sound of his praise. The sun and the stars and the moon are all pointing to him. Our imaginations must be discipled by the Word of God and the Spirit of God that we might learn to see the vision of awakening coming on the horizon—that we might join the generation of those who now labor in glad travail for its arrival.

PRAY FOR ONE ANOTHER

Lord Jesus, we want it to be said of us one day long after we have passed on into the fullness of your presence: they were oaks of righteousness. They were a planting of the Lord and their lives displayed your splendor. We want to cease living with a foot in two worlds and we want to plant both of our feet in the only true world, the one you are remaking. Give us a holy imagination to perceive it. For the sake and splendor of your name, amen.

CONFERENCE TOGETHER

One person sees a pile of rocks. The next person sees a cathedral. Which kind of person are you? Are you growing in the holiness of your imagination? Can you see yourself like a tree planted by streams of water?

DAY 23

the banner of the Bible

He said to me, "This water flows toward the eastern region and goes down into the Arabah, where it enters the Dead Sea. When it empties into the sea, the salty water there becomes fresh." (EZEK. 47:8)

The Dead Sea alive? Impossible! Next to the resurrection, this may be the most impossible feat in all of Scripture.

This river of awakening is so powerful it actually brings the Dead Sea to life. Fresh water can become salty, but it doesn't happen the other way around. Awakening means nothing less than total turn around.

There is a short declaration we see throughout Scripture that must be recovered in our time. It is one of the banners of awakening. We see it in Genesis when the angelic visitor spoke to Abraham concerning his eighty-something-year-old childless wife: "Is anything too hard for the LORD? I will return to you at the appointed time next year, and Sarah will have a son" (Gen. 18:14).

Then there was that time God instructed the prophet Jeremiah to purchase land on the eve of the catastrophic Babylonian exile, telling him that though everything would be lost, it would be returned to them. "Then the word of the LORD came to Jeremiah: 'I am the LORD, the God of all mankind. Is anything too hard for me?'" (Jer. 32:26–27).

Then there was that time the angel of the Lord visited the young teenaged girl, Mary, and told her that she would become pregnant by the Holy Spirit and give birth to the Son of God. "How will this be," Mary asked the angel, "since I am a virgin?" (Luke 1:34 ESV). The angel spoke the words, as though lifting high the great banner, "For nothing will be impossible with God" (Luke 1:37 ESV).

And let us not forget the garden of Gethsemane. At the lowest point in his earthly life, Jesus, the Son of God, literally sweating blood, cries out for a reprieve from the suffering awaiting him with these words. "'Abba, Father,' he said, 'everything is possible for you. Take this cup from me. Yet not what I will, but what you will'" (Mark 14:36).

Nothing is impossible with God. Let's call it the banner of awakening.

The Dead Sea alive? Yep!

PRAY FOR ONE ANOTHER

Come Holy Spirit and lift our eyes to the horizon of your possibilities. We renounce our cynicism, and we declare with your people at all times and in all places, nothing is impossible with you. Help us believe this—to really believe it. Yet keep us in touch with the rest of Jesus' prayer, "Not what I will, but what you will." Salt water becoming fresh. Yes, Lord. We pray in the name of the one who alone can make it so, Jesus. Amen.

CONFERENCE TOGETHER

Where have or do you put the limit on the possibility of the work of the Holy Spirit in the world? How can that limit be lifted from your thinking?

DAY 24

faith acts in anticipation
of awakening

Swarms of living creatures will live wherever the river flows. There will be large numbers of fish, because this water flows there and makes the salt water fresh; so where the river flows everything will live. (EZEK. 47:9)

It's time for some concrete thinking. What is this river of life? I think we can agree that it represents the presence, power, and love of God in the person of the Holy Spirit. We must get more concrete still. The problem with leaving it at this level of abstraction is what I call "nebulousity." We can wait years for something nebulous to happen to us before we move into action. We can pray for signs and wait for wonders as though these were the markers that what we were looking for had finally happened. Or we could move in faith. The great river of the life of the Spirit of God is moving. Pentecost is the now-open, never-closing season of the movement power of God (which is the holiness of love), flowing like a tide across the face of the earth. We only need to move with the current.

What if God is waiting for a sign from his people; that we would flash a signal of faith—not faith as easy believism, but faith as action. This is not faith, as in if we will do this then God will do that. No, it's the faith that finally moves on the reality of because God has done that, we can now do this.

Remember what Jesus said. The river of life is not something outside of us. It is the life of God within us—so where the river flows everything will live. The Holy Spirit-filled people of God are the river of life. The necessary implication of that? Everywhere the people of God go everything will live.

While this may be simple, it is not easy. It's not as simple as showing up. No, this is about growing up. More on that tomorrow.

PRAY FOR ONE ANOTHER

Father, how might we make a move of bold faith that signals to you our real belief? What would it look like to cast our nets into the deep waters? We are inquiring of you and asking you to nudge us in a direction. Show us a way. Thank you for the promise that everywhere the river goes it brings life to dead places. We believe it. We want that belief to become real faith. Come Holy Spirit! We pray in the name of the original mover, Jesus. Amen.

CONFERENCE TOGETHER

Where might your band take the river of awakening to a place in need of life? What could that look like? What holds you back?

DAY 25

from John 3:16 to 1 John 3:16

Fishermen will stand along the shore; from En Gedi to En Eglaim there will be places for spreading nets. The fish will be of many kinds—like the fish of the Mediterranean Sea. (EZEK. 47:10)

Notice the obvious here. These fishermen didn't have to find their way upriver to the source of the stream. The source came to them. They didn't need to go to church, because the church had gone to them. Jesus did not set up a headquarters and wait for the people to come. He went. And everywhere Jesus went he brought life to dead places. He was not out and about doing activities that might attract people. His was a movement of magnetic mercy.

So why do our missional activities in the world lack the irresistible magnetism of Jesus? In a word: love. It's easy enough to love helping people. It's another thing to love people. This brings us back to the challenge of our arrested adolescent faith. Helping people tends to make us feel worthwhile. Loving people makes them feel worthwhile. We all know we can help people without truly loving them but it is impossible to love them without helping them.

Helping people, which is a good thing, requires showing up. Loving people, which is a supernatural thing, necessitates growing up. Yes, this word "love" has been confused in our age. It has been confused in every age. Jesus brings crystallized clarity to its meaning.

Most of us recognize the text of John 3:16: "For God so loved the world that he gave his one and only Son, that whoever believes in him shall not perish but have eternal life." It captures the first half of the gospel. Less familiar is 1 John 3:16, which captures the essence of the second half of the gospel: "This is how we know what love is: Jesus Christ laid down his life for us. And we ought to lay down our lives for our brothers and sisters."

The journey of awakening is the Spirit-empowered, hard-fought movement of John 3:16 to 1 John 3:16. Our calling is to press on beyond adolescent faith and grow up into the maturity of love, which is nothing less than the fullness of Jesus Christ. When the people of God learn to live into 1 John 3:16, the watching world will begin to believe in John 3:16. When one generation embraces the calling into the second half of the gospel, the next generation will risk the faith to trust the first half.

One word captures this movement from Jesus' love for the world to our love for it. It is a word so visceral it defies definition. It's a word that gathers up love and life and longing into a seamless whole. The word integrates faith and action, unifies work and prayer, and joins together in an irrevocable bond the mystery of the cross and the miracle of the resurrection. The word is "travail."

Throughout history, this word has served as the watchword for awakening.

It is to that word and all it represents we now turn.

PRAY FOR ONE ANOTHER

Lord Jesus, lead us from your love for the world to our love for the world. Even better, lead us to your love for the world through us. Apart from you we are not capable of the kind of love that truly changes things, that awakens the dead. Make us people of profound love. Come Holy Spirit! We pray in your name, Jesus. Amen.

CONFERENCE TOGETHER

Do you really want to become a person of profound love; one who shares the heart of God for other people? What will this take to happen?

DAY 26

the marshes of travail

But the swamps and marshes will not become fresh; they will be left for salt. (EZEK. 47:11)

All of this movement of the river with its fresh water and swarms of living creatures and abundant fish and flourishing trees and then this curious word in verse 11 about swamps and marshes. It seems like extraneous detail and we would want to avoid overreading its significance into the text. As noted at the outset of our journey, we are reading these texts from Ezekiel with the eye of a spiritual theologian for the sake of the body of Christ. At the risk of allegory, let's explore verse 11 as it provides a lens on awakening.

A marsh is a buffer zone between two different habitats of life. Sometimes a marsh is referred to as a mire or a bog. They are muddy and wet and can only support a particular range of life-forms. Creatures made for fresh water cannot survive long in the habitat of a saltwater marsh.

Making the analogy, as a marsh is to the ecosystem of rivers and bodies of water, so is travail to the ecosystem of awakening. To travail in prayer is to stand in the gap between the kingdom of God and the kingdom of the world. It means to willingly go into the swampy territory of the place between slumber and awakening. It means to step into the miry bog of a lost and broken world and to embrace it in the love of God. To travail is to open oneself to a sharing in the divine burden for the awakening of the world.

As we said earlier, this comes back to our growing up in the love of God.

PRAY FOR ONE ANOTHER

Lord Jesus, thank you for wading from the glory of heaven into the mired bogs and marshes of this earth. Thank you for the travail of your life. Thank you for giving us a living, powerful, and beautiful example of what it looks like to love people. Forgive us for our often-anemic efforts to follow you. In fact, we can't follow you without your Spirit leading us every step of the way. Come Holy Spirit and walk us into the marshes of the world for the love of those who are still stuck there. We pray in your name, Jesus. Amen.

CONFERENCE TOGETHER

Am I ready to take more steps into the journey from John 3:16 to 1 John 3:16? What is the alternative? To stay where I am? Discuss together.

DAY 27

from sentimental nostalgia
to the travail of love

"Fruit trees of all kinds will grow on both banks of the river. Their leaves will not wither, nor will their fruit fail. Every month they will bear fruit, because the water from the sanctuary flows to them. Their fruit will serve for food and their leaves for healing." (EZEK. 47:12)

The story of Scripture opens up with the two glorious realities of light and life. The rebellion and consequent fall of the human race introduced darkness and death. The rest of Scripture's story reveals the two movements of redemption: from darkness to light and from death to life.

Left to ourselves, we are destined to the slumber of darkness and the sleep of death. By the mercy of God, we are awakened to the light of God. By the grace of God, we are awakened progressively to the life of God, and by the commission of God, we are called to become agents of awakening. We must remember that the journey of awakening, though often romanticized by history, is anything but romantic or nostalgic. Though the journey of awakening ends in a most glorious place, it begins in the shadow death and passes through many dark valleys.

The journey of awakening is not one of sentimental love but of love as glorious travail. Scripture shows us some of the contours of this travailing journey with these words: "My dear children, for whom I am again in the pains of childbirth until Christ is formed in you" (Gal. 4:19); "Now I rejoice in what I am suffering for you, and I fill up in my flesh what is still lacking in regard to Christ's afflictions, for the sake of his body, which is the church" (Col. 1:24); "We know that the whole creation has been groaning as in the pains of childbirth right up to the present time. Not only so, but we ourselves, who have the firstfruits of the Spirit, groan inwardly as we wait eagerly for our adoption to sonship, the redemption of our bodies" (Rom. 8:22–23); "In the same way, the Spirit helps us in our weakness. We do not know what we ought to pray for, but the Spirit himself intercedes for us through wordless groans. And he who searches our hearts knows the mind of the Spirit, because the Spirit intercedes for God's people in accordance with the will of God" (Rom. 8:26–27).

As the Holy Spirit travails in us, awakening us to the profound love of God, so the Spirit travails through us to make us people of profound love for others.

There may be easier journeys, but there are no greater ones.

Let's be clear. Travail is not a feature of our commitment. It is a fruit of love. We will not travail until we learn to love.

PRAY FOR ONE ANOTHER

Father, the word "travail" frightens us. It seems hard. But hard things don't seem hard when they are done in the power of your love. We confess, our own love will not cut it. We want to open our lives to you so your Spirit might travail in and through us for others. Teach us your own labor of love. We must learn this new and living way that come from you. We pray in Jesus' name, amen.

CONFERENCE TOGETHER

How do you relate to this notion of the travail of love for others? What if this is what it means to count the cost? What if the cost is our giving ourselves to the love of God for others? Discuss this today.

DAY 28

banding together to
sow for a great awakening

Thank you for taking this journey of awakening together with us. Thank you for joining a New Room Band. And thank you for banding together to sow for a great awakening. So where do we go from here?

Our hope is we can continue traveling this journey with you and your band. We have developed an ongoing approach to resourcing New Room Bands. You can find some next possible steps on the New Room Bands App. We would recommend you consider working through the short resource, *An Introduction to New Room Bands*.

Another next step would be to delve into our *Wake Up: An Introduction to the Second Half of the Gospel*. Through our research and work with people, we have discovered a tried and tested path, when walked together, bears much fruit. All most of us need is a little guidance. That's what we are offering. You will be hearing more about that in the days to come.

The pathway to an ever-deepening awakening is not an easy one and it doesn't go well alone. It may be time to launch a new band. Perhaps this first band journey was only for this season. Perhaps you want to go forward together.

Even better, perhaps you might consider each starting an additional band where you can invite others. That's how this network of bands will grow.

Small is the new big. God doesn't do in a big way what he first doesn't do in a lot of small ways. That's what this is all about—banding together to sow for a great awakening—beginning with ourselves. Awakening must begin with me.

PRAY FOR ONE ANOTHER

Lord Jesus, thank you for leading us on this journey. Thank you for showing us it is all at once easier than we thought yet harder than we imagined. Thank you for this band and their faithfulness to one another. We ask for your guidance in our next step. Show us the way we should go. We will follow. Come Holy Spirit and fill us with all the fullness of God. We pray in your name Jesus, amen.

CONFERENCE TOGETHER

What might we do as our next step?

the discipleship band meeting structure

The weekly band meeting is simple in structure and format. Budget for twenty minutes per person. Some small talk is fine, but the band must respect the time allotment. The meeting should be formally opened with the words below. Once this happens, it's band business to the end.

I. OPENING

One Voice: Awake O Sleeper and Rise from the Dead.
All Others: And Christ Will Shine on You.

(adapted from Ephesians 4:14)

PRAYER READ IN UNISON OR BY ONE MEMBER OF THE BAND

Heavenly Father, we pray that out of your glorious riches you would strengthen us with power through your Spirit in our inner being, so that Christ may dwell in our hearts through faith. And we pray that we, being rooted and established in love, may have power, together with all the Lord's holy people, to grasp how wide and long and high and deep is the love of Christ, and to know this love that surpasses knowledge—that we may be filled to the measure of all the fullness of God. We ask this in Jesus' name, amen.

(adapted from Ephesians 3:16–19)

II. THE QUESTIONS

1. How is it with your soul?
2. What are your struggles?
3. Any sin to confess?
4. Anything you want to keep secret?
5. How might the Holy Spirit be speaking and moving in your life?

In the interest of keeping it simple and memorable, think of the questions as: Soul, Struggles, Sin, Secrets, Spirit.

At the conclusion of each person's time of sharing, someone from the band will offer a prayer for the one who shared. This is also an opportunity to seek clarification, offer encouragement, and to speak into one another's lives.

It may be advisable for a new band, particularly among people unfamiliar with one another, for the first month to cover question #1 only. Perhaps add question #2 for the second month. Go at your own pace and pay attention to relational dynamics. Focus on building trust and always maintain confidentiality.

III. CLOSING

Now to him who is able to do immeasurably more than all we ask or imagine, according to his power that is at work within us, to him be glory in the church and in Christ Jesus throughout all generations, for ever and ever! Amen.

(Ephesians 3:20–21)